THE LITTLE BOOK OF
GOLF

Published by OH!
20 Mortimer Street
London W1T 3JW

Text compilation © 2020 OH!
Design © 2020 OH!

ISBN 978-1-91161-044-1

Editorial: Simon Crompton, Victoria Godden
Project Manager: Russell Porter
Design: Andy Jones
Production: Rachel Burgess

A CIP catalogue for this book is available from the British Library

Printed in Dubai

10 9 8 7 6 5 4 3 2 1

Jacket cover photograph: CHIARI VFX/Shutterstock

THE LITTLE BOOK OF
GOLF

GENERAL EDITOR
SIMON CROMPTON

CONTENTS

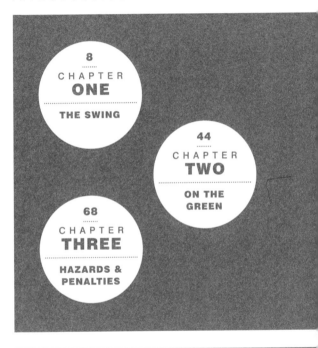

INTRODUCTION

Golfers, as author and 13-handicapper Carl Hiaasen said, love an aphorism. On course or in the clubhouse, we troll out old sayings – sometimes endlessly – to assert their truth or mock their utter fatuousness. It may or may not be true that a tree is 90% air, as some deluded and unattributed soul once said. However that doesn't mean the dodgy assertion shouldn't be quoted every time you have a woody hazard in your line.

Golf sayings are the little leitmotifs to our struggles and successes, a mental still point amid the disorientating ups and downs of a round. The quotes in this book will provide inspiration and fodder for post-round chat. They will provoke knowing nods, ridicule, laughter and bitter memories in equal measure.

Here are glib platitudes to enrage your playing partners. Here are titbits of wisdom to fill that endless and terrifying moment when you address the ball. Here are thoughts and experiences of professionals which make them seem a little bit like us.

Golfers love quotes and sayings because they can enrich our game. But they can also destroy it. George Duncan's liberating swing advice to just "go up and hit the bloody thing" is immediately liberating – and maybe experience suggests he's right. But then the great Ben Hogan also advised that the secret of a perfect swing is to "do just the opposite of what you're inclined to do". And we know he has a point too.

Thus the golfer wobbles between absolute certainty and unending doubt. That world is reflected here, particularly in the chapters on "The Swing" and "The Golfer's Mind". Golf legend Ben Crenshaw summed it up: "I'm about five inches from being an outstanding golfer. That's the distance my left ear is from my right."

In the end, golf wit and wisdom only goes to show how little any of us who play the game actually know about it. And perhaps that's why we enjoy quotations like those collected here so much: like the game itself, they are a great leveller.

Chapter

1

• • • • • • •

THE
SWING

" Golf is twenty percent mechanics and technique. The other eighty percent is philosophy, humour, tragedy, romance, melodrama, companionship, camaraderie, cussedness and conversation. **"**

GRANTLAND RICE

"When practising, use the club that gives you the most trouble, and do not waste your time in knocking the ball about with a tool that gives you the most satisfaction and with which you rarely make a bad stroke.**"**

HARRY VARDON

" The right way to play golf is to go up and hit the bloody thing. **"**

GEORGE DUNCAN

" To play good golf rests entirely on the ability to find the back of the ball with the club head square. **"**

HENRY COTTON

in 1980

"The golf ball may represent the flight of imagination but the driver reflects the baser instincts of man, the animalistic passion to dominate. I am totally addicted to my driver. It's bombs away, bombs away, bombs away. **"**

MAC O'GRADY

" Hit it hard. It will land somewhere. **"**

MARK CALCAVECCHIA

"His driving is unbelievable. I don't go that far on my holidays.**"**

IAN BAKER-FINCH

on John Daly

" If God had wanted man to play golf, he would have given him an elbowless left arm, short asymmetrical legs with side-hinged knees, and a trapezoid rib cage from which diagonally jutted a two-foot neck topped by a three-eyed head. **"**

ALAN COREN

" A bad attitude is worse than a bad swing. **"**

PAYNE STEWART

"The golfer's left side must be the dominant part of the swing. This is the only way to get maximum power and accuracy. If the right side takes over, there is no golf swing.**"**

KATHY WHITWORTH

LPGA star

" Let the ball get in the way of the swing, instead of making the ball the object. **"**

JACK BURKE SR

"First you teach a golfer to hook the ball by using his hands and arms properly. Then you teach him how to take the hook away by using his body and legs properly.**"**

HARVEY PENICK

" A golf swing is a collection of corrected mistakes. **"**

CAROL MANN

LPGA tour player

"Dividing the swing into its parts is like dissecting a cat. You'll have blood and guts and bones all over the place. But you won't have a cat.**"**

ERNEST JONES

"As far as swing and techniques are concerned, I don't know diddly squat. When I'm playing well, I don't even take aim.**"**

FRED COUPLES

❝Reverse every natural instinct you have and do just the opposite of what you're inclined to do and you will probably come very close to having a perfect golf swing.**❞**

BEN HOGAN

"Being left-handed is a big advantage.
No one knows enough about your swing to
mess you up with advice. **"**

BOB CHARLES

66 My golf swing is a bit like ironing a shirt. You get one side smoothed out, turn it over and there is a big wrinkle on the other side. Then you iron that one out, turn it over and there is yet another wrinkle. **99**

TOM WATSON

" Only one golfer in a thousand grips the clubs lightly enough. **"**

JOHNNY MILLER

"It doesn't matter if you look like a beast before or after the hit, as long as you look like a beauty at the moment of impact.**"**

SEVE BALLESTEROS

❝The more I practise, the luckier I get. **❞**

GARY PLAYER

" Got more dirt than ball. Here we go again. **"**

ALAN SHEPARD

Commander of Apollo 14, playing golf on his 1971 moon walk

"Rannulph Junuh: Anything else?
Bagger Vance: Just bash the living shit
out of it. **"**

MATT DAMON *and* **WILL SMITH**
in The Legend of Bagger Vance.

" I've never had a coach… Most people make everything far too complicated, in life as well as golf. You can pick up a club and just get on with it. **"**

LAURA DAVIES

" There was the man who seemed to be attempting to deceive his ball and lull it into a false sense of security by looking away from it and then making a lightning slash in the apparent hope of catching it off its guard. **"**

P. G. WODEHOUSE

"As for Dr. Remond Courtney, his golf swing was so unusual that from a distance he appeared to be beating a snake to death. It was a very violent golf swing for a psychiatrist."

CARL HIAASEN
Tourist Season, *1986*

❝It's much easier to have one swing
thought than many. **❞**

BUTCH HARMON

"I hit it so well on the range today I almost posted a video. Then I realised even I don't give a shit.**"**

EDDIE PEPPERELL

on Twitter, 2018

" Shanking is like the hiccups; once you start, you never know when you'll stop. **"**

CARL HIAASEN

The Downhill Lie, *2008*

"I would say it depends on what I can do in the restrictions of my biomechanics. So it's all about air, air tolerances.**"**

BRYSON DeCHAMBEAU

after a victory in 2018, when asked how much better he could get

❝I just practise before the majors.
Regular tournaments I don't practise.**❞**

BROOKS KOEPKA

at the 2019 Open in Portrush

" Yeah, I really need to work on my game. **"**

DAVID DUVAL

after scoring a record-breaking 59 at La Quinta in 1999, when asked
whether he was headed for the practice ground

❝In his book *Outliers – The Story of Success,* Malcolm Gladwell talks about the 10,000 hour rule. In effect, that to achieve mastery of a task requires practising it repeatedly for that length of time. Which means that at two hours a day of hitting balls, you should reach that target after about thirteen and a half years. And yes, this also explains why a lot of top sportsmen aren't sparkling social creatures.**❞**

ANDREW COTTER,
golf commentator, 2014

"A hybrid might rescue a player from a bad lie, but there is no rescue from a bad swing. When you suck, you suck.**"**

CARL HIAASEN

The Downhill Lie, *2008*

Chapter

2

· · · · · · ·

ON THE
GREEN

" Reading the green is like reading the small type in a contract. If you don't read it with painstaking care, you're likely to be in trouble. **"**

CLAUDE HAMILTON

"If you drink, don't drive.
Don't even putt.**"**

DEAN MARTIN

" On a putting green the mind can be a grave source of trouble. Begin to dislike the look of a putt, and the chances of holing it at once become less. **"**

JOYCE WETHERED

"The trouble with golf is you're only as good as your last putt.**"**

DOUG SANDERS

"You drive for show and putt for dough.**"**

BOBBY LOCKE

" My eyes go out of focus and my brain kind of goes out of a little focus too. So I don't get hung up on trying to hit anything on a perfect line. It's hard to explain. **"**

LOREN ROBERTS

tries to explain his touch on the green

" There is nothing so demoralising as missing a short putt. **"**

BOBBY JONES

" I enjoy the *oohs* and *aahs* from the gallery when I hit my drives, but I'm pretty tired of the *aws* and *uhhs* when I miss the putts. **"**

JOHN DALY

" It's a marriage. If I had to choose between my wife and my putter… well, I'd miss her. **"**

GARY PLAYER

❝I'm a great believer that if you don't get the ball to the hole, it won't go in.**❞**

COLIN MONTGOMERIE

"Stand them over an 18-inch putt
to win a Major and the game reverts to its
15th-century essence, the eternal puzzle of
getting a little ball into a small hole.**"**

DEREK LAWRENSON
the Daily Mail

❝I didn't think you would miss it. But I wasn't going to give you the chance.❞

JACK NICKLAUS

at the 1969 Ryder Cup, conceding a missable putt to Tony Jacklin on the final green and so halving the whole match

" No one in the world could have holed that. Jack Nicklaus wouldn't have holed it nor would Tony Jacklin. And I certainly wouldn't have holed it. **"**

SEVE BALLESTEROS

on the putt missed by Bernard Langer at the end of the 1991 Ryder Cup

"The least thing upset him on the links. He missed short putts because of the uproar of the butterflies in the adjoining meadows. **"**

P. G. WODEHOUSE

" Some weeks Nick likes to use Fanny, other weeks he prefers to do it by himself. **"**

KEN BROWN

on Nick Faldo lining up his putts. Fanny Sunesson was Faldo's caddie

❝ He's practically taken a brass-rubbing of this green. **❞**

ANDREW COTTER,

commentating on Pádraig Harrington's lengthy assessment of a birdie putt, 2008

" Bryson and I were talking about some of the science of an uphill putt and a downhill putt and the break and why it's most from this point and that point and so forth… Dustin kind of shook his head and he said, 'If I hang around you guys much longer, I'll never break 100.' **"**

PHIL MICKELSON

on a conversation with Bryson DeChambeau and Dustin Johnson during a practice round at the 2016 Masters

"It certainly puts into perspective little things like missed putts.**"**

VAN DE VELDE

on the death of Payne Stewart, 1999

"If I'd learned anything about my golf game during the past eighteen months it was this: the longer I stare at the ball, the more likely I am to botch the shot.**"**

CARL HIAASEN

considering a putt in The Downhill Lie, *2008*

"You make some stuff up in your brain, you know… What holds you back from doing your normal thing? I don't know what it is. I can go to that putting green now and make twenty straight 3-footers. And then you get on the course, and you feel a little different, and you can't do what you normally do.**"**

ERNIE ELS

trying to explain how he six-putted the first hole at the Masters, 2016

" He gave me a good talking to and told me to use a different style if it's not working. Some great advice, so I appreciate it. **"**

PGA Tour player **JEFF HERMAN**
on some putting tips provided by President Trump during the
Barbasol Championship 2019

"Stevie, my mum could've made that putt. I'm Tiger Woods – I'm supposed to make that putt. It ain't no big deal, Stevie.**"**

TIGER WOODS

to caddie Steve Williams after making a seven-foot birdie putt on the 72nd hole of the 2000 PGA Championship to get into a playoff. As reported by Williams in Out of the Rough.

Chapter

3

• • • • • • •

HAZARDS & PENALTIES

" No game demands more scientific accuracy than golf, and there is no game in which shots that are not well played more surely meet with a just punishment. **"**

JAMES BRAID

1901

" The object of a bunker or trap is not only to punish a physical mistake, to punish lack of control, but also to punish pride and egotism. **"**

CHARLES BLAIR MACDONALD

"It's a 300-acre unplayable lie.**"**

JIM MURRAY

on Pebble Beach

"If he takes the option of dropping behind the point where the ball rests, keeping in line with the pin, his nearest drop is Honolulu.**"**

JIMMY DEMARET

on Arnold Palmer looking for a drop on the 17th at Pebble Beach

" Of all the hazards, fear is the worst. **"**

SAM SNEAD

" The winner, Severiano Ballesteros, chose not to use the course but preferred his own, which mainly consisted of hay fields, car parks, grandstands, dropping zones and even ladies' clothing. **"**

COLIN MACLAINE

on Ballesteros' British Open win at Lytham in 1979

"I adore the game of golf. I won't ever retire. I'll play until I die. Then I want them to roll me into a bunker, cover me with sand and make sure nobody's ball lands in there for a while.**"**

LEE TREVINO

"When facing a hazard, focus your attention sharply on your target, not the hazard."

BOB ROTELLA

"What's the penalty for killing a photographer – one stroke or two?**"**

DAVIS LOVE III

" I give you one job to do and you can't even get that right. **"**

IAN WOOSNAM

after incurring a two-stroke penalty because his caddie packed one club too many at the 2001 British Open

"I was distracted by Jesper Parnevik's outfit. I simply couldn't believe the colour of his trousers."

MARK ROE

explains how he came to sign the wrong card in the
2003 British Open

" When we complain about conditions, we're just bitches. But when the men complain, people think, well, it really must be hard. **"**

BETSY KING

" The man who can go into a patch of rough alone with the knowledge that only God is watching him, and play his ball where it lies, is the man who will serve you faithfully and well. **"**

P. G. WODEHOUSE

"Water creates a neurosis in golfers. The very thought of this harmless fluid robs them of their normal powers of rational thought, turns their legs to jelly, and produces a palsy of the upper limbs.**"**

PETER DOBEREINER

" Golf's three ugliest words:
still your shot. **"**

DAVE MARR

" I'll take a two-shot penalty, but I'll be darned if I'm going to play the ball where it lies. **"**

ELAINE JOHNSON

after her ball hit a tree and then rebounded into her bra

" Boy, you wonder about not only the tee shot on 12, but why can't you just control the second shot and make five at worst… Big picture, this one will hurt. It will take a while. **"**

JORDAN SPIETH

after going in Rae's Creek twice and making quadruple-bogey 7 at Augusta's par 3 12th, blowing his five-shot lead at the 2016 Masters

❝It felt good at the time but now
I regret it. **❞**

RORY McILROY

*in 2015, after he'd hit the ball in the water on the 8th at Doral,
closely followed by his three-iron*

❝It's against the spirit of the game. I'm not interested in gaining an advantage in a situation like that… You just let your conscience be your guide in situations like that. **❞**

LEE WESTWOOD

at the 2019 Open, having declined a rules official's offer of a free drop for a plugged ball. Westwood said he wouldn't have had a shot from that position anyway.

❝I wasn't intentionally trying to improve a lie or anything like that.❞

PATRICK REED

after being penalised for moving sand behind his ball with practice swings in 2019

" Have you ever seen the film *Zorro?* **"**

CHRIS GANE,

English professional golfer, referring to his attempts to slash his ball out of the rough on the 18th at Gleneagles in 2003. He was in for 17.

"You never know, I might have a new endorsement with Playgirl or something like that."

HENRIK STENSON

after stripping down to his briefs to play a ball out of deep mud at the 2009 WGC-Cadillac Championship

" More than a billion golf balls are manufactured annually, and most end up lost. **"**

CARL HIAASEN

The Downhill Lie, *2008*

" I'm actually allergic to grass, trees, moss, mould and pine, all of which is rather inconvenient if you're a golfer. **"**

IAN POULTER

No Limits, *2014*

Chapter
4

• • • • • • •

THE GOLFER'S MIND

" Give me a man with big hands and big feet and no brains and I'll make a golfer out of him. **"**

WALTER HAGEN

"If I played over here four straight weeks I'd be a raving lunatic."

TOM WATSON

on the frustrations of playing golf on British links courses

❝I've learned to trust the subconscious. My instincts have never lied to me.**❞**

TIGER WOODS

" Don't lose your temper about anything — anything whatsoever. If you lose your temper, you lose everything; self-control, self-respect, judgement, equanimity, decency of language, and, of course, the hole, and probably the game. **"**

ARNOLD HAULTAIN

1910

“You play your best golf by just reacting to the target. If you are focused on the target, you aren't thinking about anything bad happening.**”**

DAVIS LOVE III

"You get to know more of the character of a man in a round of golf than in six months of political experience.**"**

DAVID LLOYD GEORGE

British statesman, Liberal MP and ex Prime Minister, Observer 1924

❝Golf books are laced with aphorisms and pithy one-line nuggets of advice because golfers aren't supposed to overload their brains. 'Swing thoughts' should be few and simple, according to the experts. One's mind should be uncluttered, and at ease. Unfortunately, the single most important fact about golf is as calming as a digital prostate exam: It's hard.**❞**

CARL HIAASEN
The Downhill Lie, *2008*

"I can tell right away if a guy is a winner or a loser just by the way he conducts himself on the course.**"**

DONALD TRUMP

66 You must attain a neurological and biological serenity in chaos. You cannot let yourself be sabotaged by adrenaline. **99**

MAC O'GRADY

"If you think positively and keep your mind on what is right, it gives you a better attitude. If you moan and groan and are disgusted, you play miserably too.**"**

BERNHARD LANGER

" I'm about five inches from being an outstanding golfer. That's the distance my left ear is from my right. **"**

BEN CRENSHAW

"I had to figure out myself to figure out my game."

STEWART CINK

" After you get the basics down,
it's all mental. **"**

KEN VENTURI

" Parasites. Everything that needs to be said about the mental side of golf could be written on a single sheet of paper. **"**

MARK JAMES

on golf psychologists

" Golf has probably kept more people sane than psychiatrists have. **"**

HARVEY PENICK

"Instead of putting pressure on myself and thinking, 'I've got to make this shot', I just thought, 'Go ahead and make it'. It's a subtle difference but a big one."

COREY PAVIN

on holing a nine iron in the 1993 Ryder Cup

" The trouble with me is I think too much. I always said you have to be dumb to play good golf. **"**

JoANNE CARNER

LPGA golfer

"I never take myself too seriously.**"**

LEE WESTWOOD

"Thinking must be the hardest thing we do in golf, because we do so little of it.**"**

HARVEY PENICK

❝You don't win tournaments by playing well and thinking poorly. **❞**

LEE WESTWOOD

"I have mostly been eating chicken wings. I only stick to things I can spell.**"**

BOO WEEKLEY

on his diet at the 2009 Open

"You're trying to take souls. You're going there to make people cry at this point, just crush the other team. That's the fun of it.**"**

LPGA golfer **DANIELLE KANG**

in the build-up to the 2019 Solheim Cup

Chapter

5

· · · · · · · ·

IN
COMPETITION

"A mullet par excellence, big, blond and deeply unfashionable… an all-American mission statement that said I'm from Arkansas and I don't give a shit.**"**

GAVIN NEWSTON

in John Daly: The Biography

" My most common mistake at
St Andrews is turning up. **"**

MARK JAMES

" Carnoustie Golf Club, Scotland: a good swamp, spoiled. **"**

GARY PLAYER

" Winning isn't everything, but wanting to is. **"**

ARNOLD PALMER

❝The only time I talk on a golf course is to my caddie. And then only to complain when he gives me the wrong club. **❞**

SEVE BALLESTEROS

" The best feeling of all? …you are in your room on your own and you stare at the ceiling and say to yourself: *By God, I beat the lot of them. I really did beat them all*. That's the real moment to savour. **"**

TONY JACKLIN

" Play every shot as if it's the first shot you're ever going to play. The tournament starts on the next shot you hit. **"**

GREG NORMAN

"Always throw clubs ahead of you. That way you don't have to waste energy going back to pick them up.**"**

TOMMY BOLT

❝I look into their eyes, shake their hand, pat their back, and wish them luck, but I'm thinking, I'm going to bury you.**❞**

SEVE BALLESTEROS

" Every golfer has a little monster in him,
it's just that type of sport. **"**

FUZZY ZOELLER

"The most exquisitely satisfying act in the world of golf is that of throwing a club. The full backswing, the delayed wrist action, the flowing follow-through, followed by that unique whirring sound, reminiscent only of a passing flock of starlings, are without parallel in sport. **"**

HENRY LONGHURST

"Golf is the hardest game in the world. There's no way you could ever get it. Just when you think you do, the game jumps up and puts you in your place.**"**

BEN CRENSHAW

"The toughest thing for most people to learn in golf is to accept bad holes – and then forget about them.**"**

GARY PLAYER

"I played crap, he played crap. He just out-crapped me."

WAYNE GRADY

after losing the 1990 World Matchplay championship to Greg Norman

"I don't know what to say. I just want to give you a hug.**"**

NICK FALDO

to Greg Norman, after Norman lost a six shot lead in the final round of the 1996 US Masters

❝Talking to a golf ball won't do you any good. Unless you do it while your opponent is teeing off. **❞**

BRUCE LANSKY

" Be patient. You know exactly how to play this course. You are the greatest golfer in the world. **"**

SEVE BALLESTEROS,

*in a note given to José María Olazábal before the final round
of the 1994 Masters*

" Don't tell the opponent to drive first when you have won the toss for the honour. It is a confession of weakness. **"**

H. L. FITZPATRICK

1900

❝Stroke play is a better test of golf, but matchplay is a better test of character.**❞**

JOE CARR

" Golfing excellence goes hand-in-hand with alcohol, as many an Open and amateur champion has shown. **"**

CHARLES PRICE

on leading a golf tournament

"I've had my son crying sometimes. He says: 'You never let me win!' But there's no point because it doesn't mean anything. The satisfaction you get when you finally beat your dad is amazing, that rush of adrenaline.**"**

LEE WESTWOOD

talking to The Guardian, *2010*

"Even the rust is rusty."

SIR NICK FALDO

after his final round at the Open, 2015. He posted a second-round 71

after a first-round 11 over par.

"I wouldn't say that we go way back. I played one practice round with him at Wells Fargo a couple years ago.**"**

HENRIK STENSON

after being told that Patrick Reed had named him as his friend on tour in 2018

I've seen nicer rings in Ann Summers.

EDDIE PEPPERELL

responding to Bubba Watson's tweet proudly displaying the commemorative Ryder Cup ring presented to every member of the American team, September 2018

❝Shit. Do you want me to elaborate?
Really shit. **❞**

DANNY WILLETT

when asked about his 2016 Ryder Cup experience: Europe lost and Willett had been heckled by American fans following an abrasive piece written by his brother.

"If he couldn't chip, he'd be selling cars in San Diego."

JOHNNY MILLER

on Phil Mickelson's scrambling skills at the 2010 Ryder Cup

" This is some crappy golf. I could beat these two today. **"**

CHARLES BARKLEY,
sports commentator, on 'The Match' between Tiger Woods and Phil Mickelson, 2018

"One of my biggest goals is to try to get into the top 1,000 of the World Ranking. If I can sneak my way into the top 1,000, that'd be a great goal.**"**

TIGER WOODS

in 2016. He won the Masters in 2019.

❝I think I'm going to do exactly the same thing I did on Friday night. I'm going to have a margarita as an aperitif, and then I'm going to have a nice bottle of Rioja and smoke a big fat cigar.**❞**

MIGUEL ÁNGEL JIMÉNEZ

on his routine the night before he won his first Senior Major in 2018

"Everybody has something – some sort of handshake, a fist bump, a tap on the hiney. I figured this was a good opportunity for me to slap Bubba in the face.**"**

MATT KUCHAR

on his celebration routine with partner Bubba Watson at the Zurich Classic, 2018

" Enjoy your day, buddy. You're gone. **"**

JUSTIN THOMAS

as he had a heckler removed during the final round of the
Honda Classic 2018

"I literally can't tell you what happened during those holes. You kind of black out. Everything is so repetitive."

BROOKS KOEPKA

before the 2019 USPGA, revealing he gets bored in the middle of a round

❝I don't know, I've never played there.**❞**

SANDY LYLE

asked by a reporter what he thought of Tiger Woods in 1995.
Woods was, in fairness, still an amateur.

❝I promised myself to make an eagle but I tried too hard.❞

TOMMY NAKAJIMA

after making a 13 on the 13th at Augusta National in 1978

❝Certainly not built for speed.**❞**

KEN BROWN

commentating on J. B. Holmes during the 2019 Open, after a fellow pundit commented on Holmes' sturdy build. Holmes had been widely criticised for slow play.

❝Tiger, you have to absolutely trust me on this one. And if I'm wrong, fire me. I know how much this means to you, so if I'm wrong just fire me.**❞**

STEVE WILLIAMS,

caddie to Tiger Woods, before Woods' third shot to the 72nd hole of the 2008 US Open at Torrey Pines. Woods won. As reported by Williams in Out of the Rough.

Chapter

6

· · · · · · ·

GOLF
& LIFE

❝Golf is deceptively simple, endlessly complicated. A child can play it well, and a grown man can never master it.**❞**

ROBERT FORGAN

1899

"It is not a matter of life and death. It is not that important. But it is a reflection of life, and so the game is an enigma wrapped in a mystery impaled on a conundrum.**"**

PETER ALLISS

" Never hurry, never worry, and always remember to smell the flowers along the way. **"**

WALTER HAGEN

"What a beautiful place a golf course is. From the meanest country pasture to the Pebble Beaches and St Andrewses of the world, a golf course is to me holy ground. I feel God in the trees and grass and flowers, in the rabbits and the birds and the squirrels, in the sky and the water. I feel that I am home.**"**

HARVEY PENICK

" The road's getting shorter and narrower, but I'll play wherever the pigeons land. **"**

SAM SNEAD

at eighty-one

" If there is one thing golf demands above all else, it is honesty. **"**

JACK NICKLAUS

"All my life I wanted to play like Jack Nicklaus, and now I do.**"**

PAUL HARVEY,

legendary radio broadcaster, after the Golden Bear shot an 83
in the 1981 British Open

66 The older you get the stronger the wind gets and it's always in your face. 99

JACK NICKLAUS

" I am still young. When I'm older there will be time to be careful. **"**

SEVE BALLESTEROS

after finishing runner-up in the 1976 British Open

66 People are always telling me I should do one thing or another. I should change my grip or shorten my swing. I should practise more and goof around less. I shouldn't smile on Sunday – I should – I shouldn't – frankly, I don't know why they worry. It's my life – and I don't worry. **99**

FRED COUPLES

" Golf is a puzzle without an answer.
I've played golf for 40 years and I still haven't
the slightest idea how to play. **"**

GARY PLAYER

❝That's a stupid question.**❞**

CRAIG STADLER

in 2015 when asked whether his Green Jacket from 1982 still fits

"I started drinking four years after I started playing golf. And I started playing golf when I was four.**"**

JOHN DALY

"That was a great game of golf, fellas.""

BING CROSBY

his last words after collapsing at La Moraleja golf course, Spain, 1977

" Golf is not a sport – it's an artistic exercise like ballet. You can be a fat slob and still play golf. **"**

JOHN McENROE

❝I've had a bad week. But in the real world, having a bad week is waking up and finding you're a steelworker in Scunthorpe. **❞**

NICK FALDO

after a poor Ryder Cup in 1991

" Golf is the cruellest of sports. Like life, it's unfair. It's a harlot, a trollop. It leads you on. It never lives up to its promises. It's not a sport, it's bondage. An obsession. A boulevard of broken dreams. It plays with men. And runs off with the butcher. **"**

JIM MURRAY

" Losing this Masters is not the end of the world. I let this one get away, but I still have a pretty good life. I'll wake up tomorrow still breathing, I hope. **"**

GREG NORMAN

after losing a six-stroke lead to Nick Faldo on the final round of the 1996 Masters

" It's the most humbling sport ever. It's like a lousy lover. It's like some guy who's never there when you need him. Every once in a while, he comes and makes you feel like heaven on earth. And then the moment you say, 'I really need this', he's gone. **"**

DINAH SHORE

" Golf is a game to be played between cricket and death. **"**

COLIN INGLEBY-MACKENZIE

" Golf is a day spent in a round of strenuous idleness. **"**

WILLIAM WORDSWORTH

"The only way of really finding out a man's true character is to play golf with him. In no other walk of life does the cloven hoof so quickly display itself.**"**

P. G. WODEHOUSE

" I never pray on a golf course. Actually, the Lord answers my prayers everywhere except on the course. **"**

REV BILLY GRAHAM

American evangelist preacher

"All games are silly, but golf,
if you look at it dispassionately, goes
to extremes.**"**

PETER ALLISS

" A typical day in the life of a
heavy metal musician consists of a round of
golf and an AA meeting. **"**

BILLY JOEL

" Golf was my first glimpse of comedy. I was a caddie when I was a kid. I was on the golf course rather than being in lessons, but I can play better now than I could then. **"**

BILL MURRAY

"We had a big conversation at the end of the year last year, and he didn't like it. I said: 'You gotta decide, are you going to be a Kardashian or are you going to be a golf pro?'**"**

BUTCH HARMON

on Rickie Fowler, 2017

❝All men die but not all men
live and you made me feel alive again
this week. **❞**

JOSÉ MARÍA OLAZÁBAL,
*Europe Captain, on his team's superb performance in the Ryder Cup
at Medinah in 2012*

❝Francesco and Tommy have gotten awfully close this week so I don't know what's going to happen between them tonight. **❞**

RORY McILROY

McIlroy on the bromance between Tommy Fleetwood and Francesco Molinari who won four out of four together at the Ryder Cup 2018

"What can I say? I love him. We enjoy playing together, and spending time together. **"**

FRANCESCO MOLINARI

on Ryder Cup partner Tommy Fleetwood, 2018

" In Sainsbury's, looking for mashed potatoes and rubber gloves – Marigolds, small size. **"**

LEE WESTWOOD

in 2010, when asked how he found out he had become the world's number one golfer

"Golf balls don't know how old you are. "

PAUL LAWRIE,
former Open champion, on Tom Watson's week at Turnberry in 2009,
when he nearly won the Open aged fifty-nine

❝ That's a very easy question, it would be the three wood. **❞**

HENRIK STENSON

responding without a beat when asked to choose (hypothetically)
between his wife and his three wood

" He is a quiet, thoughtful, respectful guy. And I'm not, which is probably why we hit it off so well. **"**

IAN POULTER

on Justin Rose, No Limits, *2014*

❝Maybe I'm going to blow it but I'm going to enjoy it even if I do.**❞**

JEAN VAN DE VELDE

as he went into the final round of the Open at Carnoustie with a five-shot lead in 1999. He blew it, making a triple bogie on the 18th and losing out to Paul Lawrie in the play-off.

192